AF584428

Famous Australians

Australians at the Olympic Games

Rachel Dixon

First published 2017 by
Redback Publishing
PO Box 357 Frenchs Forest NSW 2086
Australia

ISBN 978-1-9256301-7-6

Author: Rachel Dixon
Editor: Jane Hinchey
Original illustrations © Redback Publishing 2017
Originated by Redback Publishing
Printed and bound in China by Leo Paper

Acknowledgements
Abbreviations: l—left, r—right, b—bottom, t—top, c—centre, m—middle
We would like to thank the following for permission to reproduce photographs: State Library of New South Wales, http://freeaussiestock.com, P4 (Dawn Fraser) Eva Rinaldi, P5 Jason Pini/AusAID, P9 TSGT Rick Sforza, P10b PA Images / Alamy Stock Photo, p21t Keystone Pictures USA / Alamy Stock Photo, P15 HowardMorland, P16 Adam.JWC, P16 Adam.JWC, P17 Kookaburradreaming, P19 Ken Hackman, U.S. Air Force, P19 Pixeltoo, updated by Zscout370, P22 Meyer Albert (1857 - 1924) Details of artist on Google Art Project, P23 National Media Museum from UK, P23 Australian National Maritime Museum - via Wikimedia Commons. p15 AA World Travel Library / Alamy Stock Photo

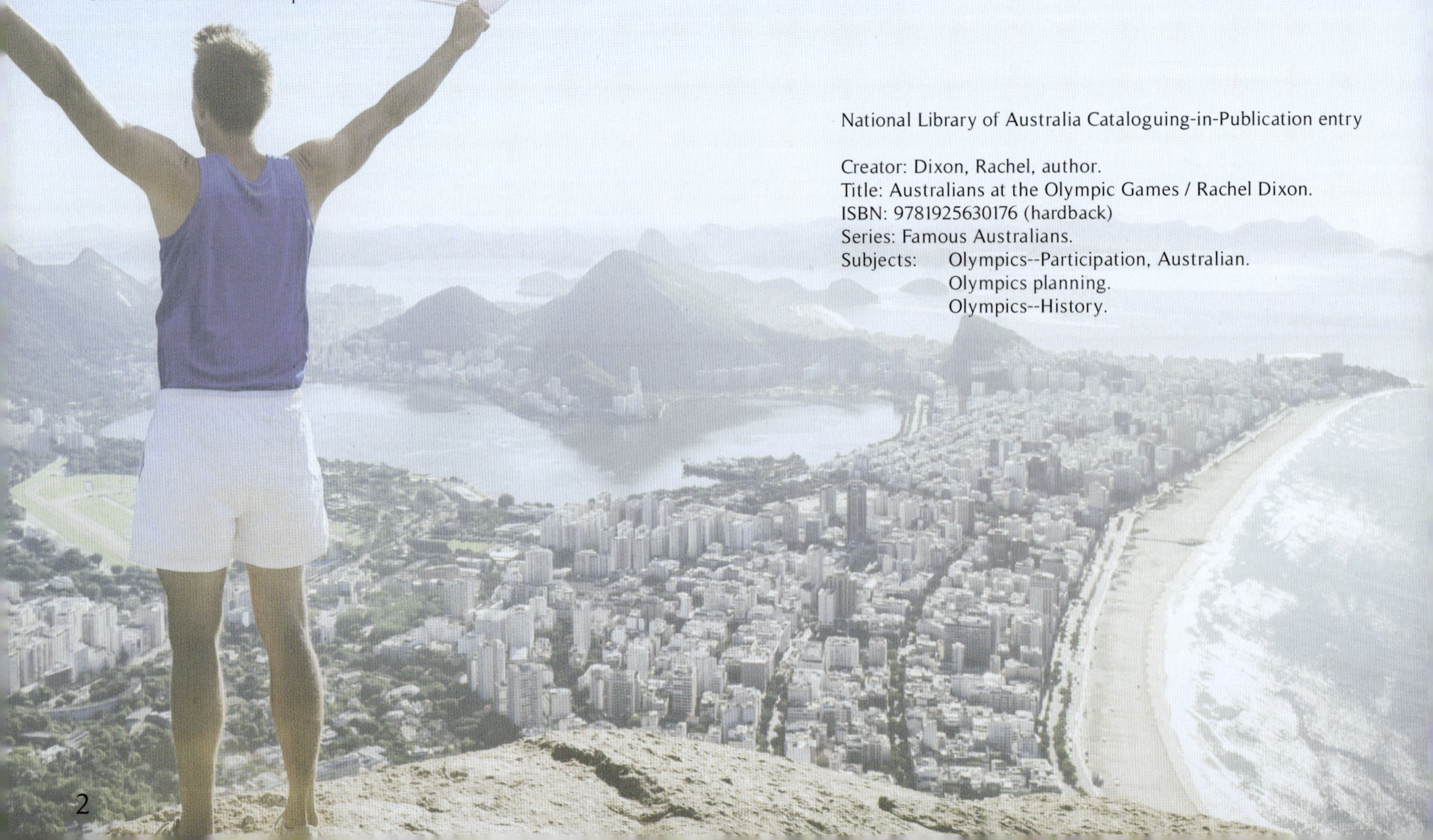

National Library of Australia Cataloguing-in-Publication entry

Creator: Dixon, Rachel, author.
Title: Australians at the Olympic Games / Rachel Dixon.
ISBN: 9781925630176 (hardback)
Series: Famous Australians.
Subjects: Olympics--Participation, Australian.
Olympics planning.
Olympics--History.

Contents

Australia's Greatest Olympic Gold Medallists

Ian Thorpe - 5 Gold Medals

Ian Thorpe was born in 1982 in Sydney. He started swimming in competitions when he was eight years old and, at fourteen, was the youngest swimmer ever to become a member of the Australian swimming team. At the 2000 and 2004 Olympics, and at the World Swimming Championships, he showed that he was an outstanding athlete, winning gold medals and breaking records. His nickname was The Thorpedo, because of his fast and smooth swimming style. Retiring from swimming in 2011, Ian Thorpe remains the Olympian who has won the most gold medals for Australia.

Above: Ian Thorpe

Betty Cuthbert - 4 Gold Medals

Betty Cuthbert was born in 1938 in Sydney. She won three gold medals in running at the Melbourne Olympics in 1956 and then another gold medal at the 1964 Tokyo Olympics. Nicknamed Australia's Golden Girl, Betty Cuthbert was diagnosed with Multiple Sclerosis in 1969. Since then, she has campaigned to raise funds for the Multiple Sclerosis Society.

Above: Dawn Fraser

Dawn Fraser - 4 Gold Medals

Named World Athlete of the Century, Dawn Fraser was a swimming sensation with her gold medal wins and record-breaking efforts. Born in Balmain, Sydney in 1937, she became the first woman in the world to win gold medals for swimming in three consecutive Olympic Games, starting with the Melbourne Olympics in 1956. She was later elected a member of the New South Wales Parliament and continues her work for various sporting organisations.

Libby Trickett - 4 Gold Medals

Born in Townsville, Queensland in 1985, Libby Trickett won gold medals in swimming over three consecutive Olympic Games, starting in 2004. She set a number of records in the 100 metres freestyle, and won many World Championships. Libby has also been a television presenter and works for various charities. In 2005, she was awarded the Order of Australia Medal.

Murray Rose - 4 Gold Medals

Murray Rose was born in England in 1939 and brought to Australia by his parents when he was a baby. He and Ian Thorpe are the only two swimmers ever to have won the 400 metres freestyle swimming at two consecutive Olympics. He had already won four Olympic gold medals when he was controversially excluded from the 1964 Olympic Games in Tokyo due to not swimming in the Australian Championships earlier. Murray Rose died in 2012.

Shane Gould - 3 Gold Medals

Shane Gould was born in 1956 in Sydney. In 1972, when she was only seventeen years old, Gould held every freestyle swimming world record. She competed at the 1972 Munich Olympics, winning five individual Olympic medals, including three gold. Despite this remarkable achievement, she withdrew from international competition to concentrate on higher education and her environmental and charitable projects.

Grant Hackett - 3 Gold Medals

Grant Hackett was born on the Gold Coast, Queensland in 1980. Adding together his medal wins across all competitions, Grant Hackett is one of Australia's most awarded athletes of all time. He represented Australia in swimming across three Olympic Games, and his numerous awards include an Order of Australia Medal. After retiring from competition he spent time as a television sports presenter.

Above: Grant Hackett

Above: Shane Gould

Shirley Strickland - 3 Gold Medals

Shirley Strickland was born in Guildford, Western Australia in 1925. She won three gold medals in hurdles and relay and represented Australia at three Olympic Games. For many years there was a dispute over whether she had won a bronze medal or not in the 200 metres at London in 1948. At the time, she was judged to have finished fourth, but in 1975 a photo of the finish line was discovered showing her coming third. Shirley Strickland gained an honours degree in nuclear physics and lectured in physics and mathematics. She died in 2004.

Marjorie Jackson - 2 Gold Medals

Marjorie Jackson was born in Lithgow, New South Wales in 1931 and became known as The Lithgow Flash. She won two gold medals at the Helsinki Games in 1952 and was the first Australian woman to win an Olympic gold medal in athletics. After retiring from athletics she had a distinguished career, becoming the Governor of South Australia in 2001.

Cathy Freeman - 1 Gold Medal

Cathy Freeman was born in 1973 in Mackay, Queensland. She is remembered fondly by Australians for her emotional gold medal win in the 400 metres sprint at the Sydney Olympics in 2000. All across the nation people stopped what they were doing to watch her run this race. This was Australia's one hundredth Olympic gold medal. In 1998 she was Australian of the Year, and in 2001 she was awarded the Olympic Order from the IOC. As well as her Olympic gold medal, Cathy Freeman has also won gold at the Commonwealth Games four times and at the World Championships twice.

Below: Cathy Freeman

History of the Olympic Games

Ancient Olympic Games

The first Olympic Games were held in Olympia in 776 BC. They were organised to honour Zeus, the king of the gods.

The Games were held amongst athletes from the cities of Greece. Only men were allowed to compete, and the best overall sportsman was crowned with a wreath of olive leaves. They had to be free Greek citizens, but rich and poor could enter the competition. Married women were not allowed to watch the Games, but unmarried ones could.

Above: Ruins at Olympia

DID YOU KNOW?

No-one in ancient Greece knew that the continent of Australia existed, although a few people thought that there was probably a large land mass somewhere in the southern oceans.

Thousands of people went to Olympia to see the Games, just as people travel to cities holding the Olympics today. They watched athletes compete in events such as running, wrestling, the long jump, disc throwing and javelin throwing.

The Olympic Games were banned in 393 AD, when the Roman Emperor outlawed all worship of the ancient gods.

Modern Olympic Games

In the 1890s, Baron Pierre de Coubertin gathered support for the Olympic Games to be held again. The first modern Games were held in Athens in 1896 and Australia was one of the fourteen nations to have a competitor. The notion of international friendship based on sporting competition has been an ideal connected with the Olympics from ancient to modern times.

WHAT DO YOU THINK?

- Does playing sport encourage friendship between the players?
- What are some differences between the ancient and modern Olympic Games?
- Does the success of athletes at the Olympics encourage other people to take up sport for health and fitness?

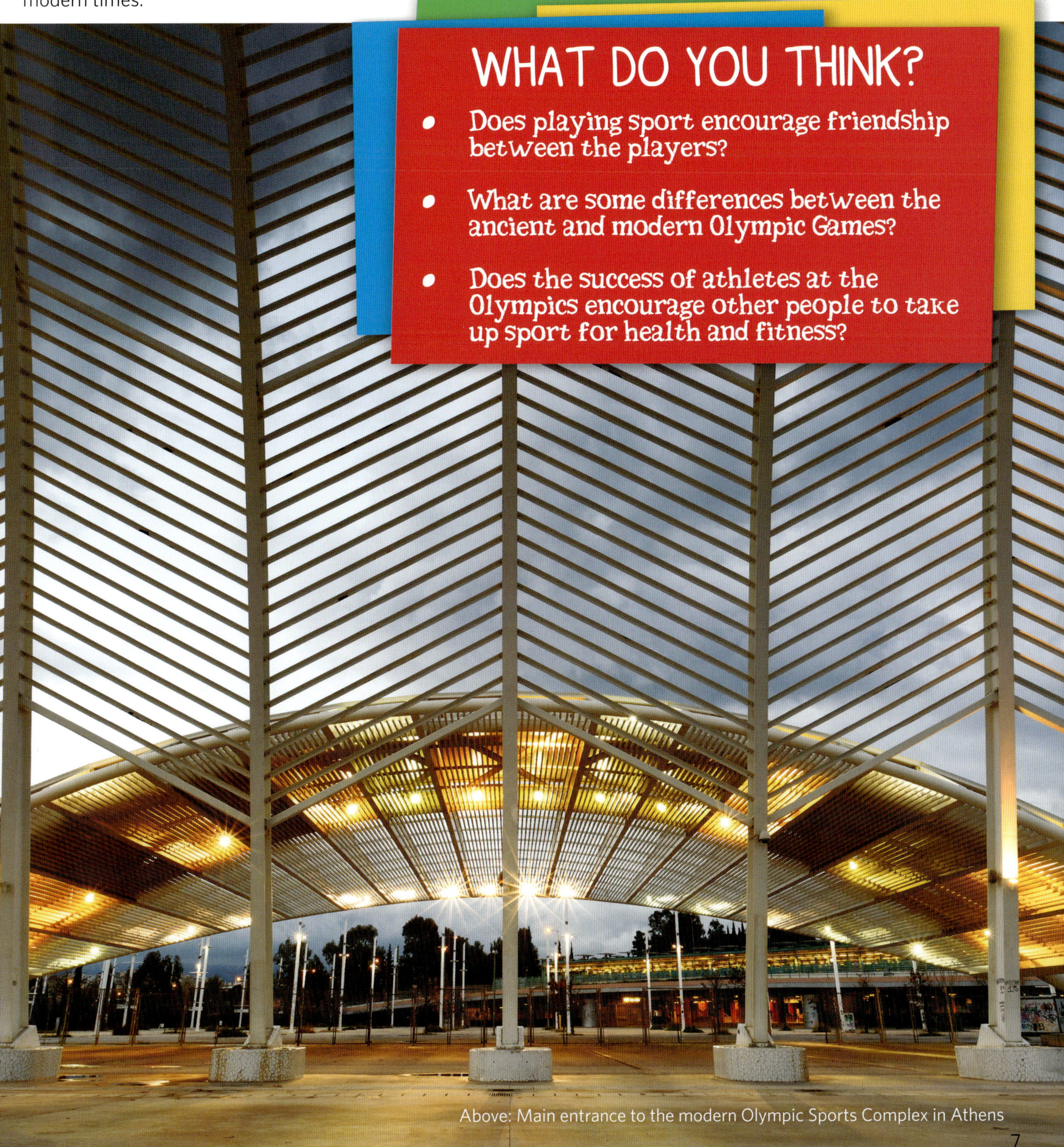

Above: Main entrance to the modern Olympic Sports Complex in Athens

Symbols of the Olympic Games

Olympic Rings

The five interlinked rings represent the five continents of the world. The order of the colours, from left to right, is blue, yellow, black, green and red. Every nation of the world had at least one of these colours on its own flag when the symbol was designed in 1913.

Olympic Flag

The Olympic flag has the five rings on a white background. It was first flown in the Olympic Games in Belgium in 1920.

DID YOU KNOW?

The original Olympic flag was lost for years until a 101 year old former athlete revealed he had souvenired it in 1920. The first flag is now on display in the Olympic Museum in Switzerland.

Sydney 2000 Olympic Torch Relay

The torch relay in Australia in 2000 began at Uluru, continued underwater through the Great Barrier Reef and ended with Cathy Freeman lighting the cauldron in Sydney. There were a few moments of suspense when the cauldron refused to light, but the flames eventually rose and Cathy was praised afterwards for remaining so calm.

Above: Olympic torch 2013

Olympic Torch Relay and Flame

The flame is an ancient symbol of purity that was used in Greek temples. Before the Olympic Games begin every four years, the flame is relit at Olympia in Greece, using only the sun's rays. Women representing the ancient priestesses then light the torch of the first relay runner. Each torch is used to light the next runner's torch in sequence. Finally, the last runner brings the torch into the Olympic Games arena and lights a cauldron. The flame burns throughout the Games and is extinguished at the closing ceremony.

Below: Olympic rings on Olympic flag

FAST FACT

The Olympic torch was kept alight underwater on the Great Barrier Reef using a converted marine flare.

Olympic Motto

'Citius, Altius, Fortius', which is Latin for 'Faster, Higher, Stronger'.

Opening and Closing Ceremonies

These ceremonies began as simple marches by the athletes and speeches by officials. Gradually more entertainment was introduced and now these ceremonies are major theatrical events. Journalists report on the standard of the ceremonies, and each country's production is compared with that of countries that have held the Olympics before them.

For the Sydney Olympics in 2000, millions of Australians watched the televised ceremonies, and were enthralled by the music and drama of the presentations. Because the stage used for the ceremonies was so large, the expert skills of engineers and technicians were needed, as well as the design and creativity skills of the artistic directors and performers.

Olympic Music

The Olympic anthem has been performed at every opening and closing ceremony since 1960. The music was written by Spyridon Samaras for the first modern Olympics in 1896. John Williams later composed an Olympic fanfare for the 1984 Games in Los Angeles.

HAS ANY COUNTRY TOPPED THIS?

In Barcelona in 1992, an archer lit the cauldron by firing a flaming arrow across the stadium.

Olympic Mascots

The first official mascots were created for the Munich Games in 1972. The mascots for the Sydney Games in 2000 were Syd (a platypus), Olly (a kookaburra) and Millie (an echidna). The mascots' names refer to the words Sydney, Olympic and millennium.

Below: Sydney Olympic Stadium: Opening ceremony for the 2000 Olympic Games

Melbourne Olympic Games 1956

The first Olympic Games held in the Southern Hemisphere were in Melbourne in 1956. They were also the first to use television to allow people around the world to see the events.

The main stadium was built in an upgraded Melbourne Cricket Ground, and the gold medal tally for Australia was outstanding for a country with a small population. With thirty-five medals, Australia was third on the medal tally behind the USSR and the USA. The local stars of the Games were Dawn Fraser, Betty Cuthbert, Shirley Strickland and Murray Rose.

Equestrian Events

The equestrian events could not be held in Melbourne because there was not enough time for imported horses to be in quarantine to ensure they were not bringing diseases into the country. The horse riding events had to be held in Stockholm for those Games. The Australian team came fourth in eventing in 1956, and in later Olympics built on this success to become medal winners.

Right: Equestrian event at the Olympics
Below: Melbourne Olympic Games 1956

Above: Melbourne Olympic Games 1956
Left: Postage stamp for the 1956 Melbourne Olympic Games

Visitors

Melbourne had never hosted an event of this size before, and there were not enough hotels for all the visitors. Residents were asked to take visitors into their homes and provide board and breakfast. The homes were inspected for their suitability and the owners were quizzed on their way of life, so that visitors could be matched with people who were as similar to them as possible.

The Friendly Games

The Melbourne Olympics became known as the Friendly Games. The tradition of all athletes marching together at the closing ceremony, rather than as separate teams, began at these Olympics.

Above: Emblem for the Melbourne Olympic Games

Sydney
Olympic Games 2000

When the Sydney Olympics were over, Australians were proud to hear the president of the International Olympic Committee declare that they had been 'the best Olympic Games ever'. Australia achieved its highest medal tally at these Games, with sixteen gold, twenty-five silver and seventeen bronze.

Do you know someone who was a volunteer at the Sydney Olympic Games in 2000?

Can you find their name on the Games Memories poles at Sydney Olympic Park?

Volunteers

An army of 47,000 volunteers was organised to help the thousands of visitors. These volunteers' names are now recorded on a special memorial at Sydney Olympic Park.

Below: Sydney Olympic Stadium 2000

Below: Cathy Freeman

Venues

Sydney Olympic Park was the main location for the sporting events, although some competitions were held at other venues. Volleyball was held at Bondi Beach, equestrian events at the Sydney International Equestrian Centre and canoeing at the Penrith Whitewater Stadium.

Highlights

Cathy Freeman was the undoubted star of these Olympics. She lit the cauldron at the opening ceremony and, after her gold medal win, ran a victory lap draped in the Australian and Aboriginal flags.

The crowds also cheered for Eric Moussambani, nicknamed Eric the Eel, from Equatorial Guinea. Despite coming last and swimming a very slow race, the crowd admired his courage at competing for his country, which did not even have any public swimming pools.

Medals

Australia designed its own medals for the 2000 Olympics. The Goddess of Victory is shown on one side, and the Opera House on the other. The medals were made at the Royal Australian Mint in Canberra and designed by Polish-Australian artist Wojciech Pietranik. The gold medals were not actually made from pure gold, but from gold-plated silver.

The emblem suggests an athlete, the Opera House and the first inhabitants of Australia.

FIND OUT FOR YOURSELF

Do you know anyone who remembers the Sydney Olympic Games in 2000?

Ask them what the most memorable event was for them.

Aboriginal history of Sydney Olympic Park at Homebush Bay

Timeline

10,000 years ago	At the end of the last Ice Age, rising sea levels submerged much of Sydney's coast, including the valley that once existed where Homebush Bay is now. Aboriginal people living in the area would have moved to higher ground as the water rose. The submerged Parramatta River and its creeks now form the Homebush Bay waterways.
Before 1788	The land at Homebush Bay belonged to the Wann-gal people. The water frontages were thick with mangroves and had wide mud flats. Throughout this area archaeologists have found stone tools and scarred trees, whose bark was peeled to make implements and canoes.
After 1788	Land at Homebush Bay was granted to colonial settlers, resulting in conflict between them and the Wann-gal people.

Olympic Games and Economics

Although the world focuses on the athletes during each Olympics, there is much more to the Games than sporting excellence.

Funding the Olympics

The city that hosts the Olympics hopes to raise the whole nation's profile internationally, resulting in increases in tourism and investment. There is a high cost involved in building the venues and accommodation for the sporting teams, as well as ensuring that there is sufficient public transport and adequate facilities for thousands of visitors. The governments providing the funds for these projects expect that there will be an economic advantage to the country as a result.

Showcasing the Host City

Magnificent purpose-built venues showcase the architectural and engineering expertise available in the host city. The talents displayed in the opening and closing ceremonies alert the world to the performance and artistic skills that people from the host city possess. All of these can contribute to future business opportunities and income for the country holding the Olympic Games. On the other hand, poor organisation of the Olympic Games can have a detrimental effect on a nation's international image.

Choosing the Host City for the Olympic Games

The International Olympic Committee (IOC) in Switzerland chooses the cities that will host the Olympic Games. One of the important things they consider before making a choice is whether the city is economically able to provide all the buildings and infrastructure needed to run the Games. Winning cities are announced seven years before their Games are to be held.

THINK ABOUT IT

Are there any community groups or businesses that would not want to have the Olympic Games in their city?

Why might they be opposed to hosting the Games?

Above: Beijing Water Cube hosted swimming and diving events at the Olympics

Above: White Water Stadium at Penrith

THINK ABOUT IT

Can you think of three types of businesses that would benefit from having the Olympic Games in their city?

Observer Program

The IOC seeks to ensure that the Olympic Games leave a 'positive, longterm and sustainable legacy' for the city hosting them. To help achieve this aim, the IOC runs an Observer Program for representatives of cities that want to hold the Games in the future. This lets them see how the next Olympic Games are being organised. They investigate everything from ticketing and transport to building and finances.

After the Olympic Games in Sydney

- The main location for the 2000 Sydney Olympic Games was Sydney Olympic Park. The precinct is twice the size of the Sydney Central Business District and after the Games it became a centre for exhibitions, sport, recreation and business. There is also a large residential development. Sydney Olympic Park is now the venue for the Royal Easter Show, the largest annual event held in Australia.
- Sydney has benefitted from the Olympic Games by having sporting venues which it did not possess before. An example is the Penrith Whitewater Stadium, which is an artificial river that is now used for recreation and sporting competitions.
- Tourists from other parts of Australia and from around the world have decided to visit Sydney as a result of seeing it on television during the Olympics.

Sustainability and the Environment at the Olympic Games

The Melbourne Olympic Games 1956

Although ideas about the environment and sustainability were different in 1956 than they are today, the organisers were very careful to ensure that Australia was not exposed to imported diseases that could damage local livestock industries. The quarantine rules for the importation of horses were not relaxed for the Melbourne Olympics, which meant that the equestrian events could not be held in Australia. The competitions involving horses were held in Stockholm instead.

The Sydney Olympic Games 2000

Organisers of these Games used the term The Green Games to emphasise the importance placed on preservation of the environment and a commitment to sustainability.

Below: Sydney Olympic Park at dusk, streets lined with solar powered lighting

Above: Cumberland Plain Woodland

The main site for the events had been an industrial area. The creeks running through it were polluted and the land had to be managed so that any waste did not contaminate the new development. Environmental improvements were achieved using the following methods:

- Water recycling - Sewage and stormwater were recycled for gardens and toilet flushing.
- Solar energy - The Olympic Village was powered by solar cells on every roof.
- Pollution control - Creeks entering the precinct needed litter control booms to stop rubbish being washed downstream.
- Biodiversity - The area was home to many species of wildlife and their habitats were preserved.
- Parks - The industrial wastelands were converted into parks and wildlife refuges.
- Dangerous waste - Some wastes were buried and any liquid coming from them was treated in a complex system of drains, pumps and treatment ponds.
- Volunteers - Volunteers today are encouraged to help survey wildlife and to assist with regular clean-ups of the extensive parklands and waterways.

Below: Green and Golden Bell Frogs are thriving at Olympic Park

Above: Sydney Olympic Park wetlands

Unlike the Melbourne Olympics in 1956, the Sydney Olympics in 2000 had no problems staging the equestrian events. Horses came to Sydney on chartered flights and were quarantined at the Sydney International Equestrian Centre. Improvements in veterinary testing since 1956 meant that in 2000 there was much less risk of diseases that could threaten local livestock being brought into Australia.

Politics and the Olympic Games

When Pierre de Coubertin founded the modern Olympic Games, he hoped they would be based on the ancient Athenian ideal that all wars would stop while the Games were underway. In the modern world the opposite was true. The Olympic Games were cancelled during both World Wars, in 1916 and then again in 1940 and 1944.

Belgium 1920

When the Olympics were run in 1920 in Belgium, after World War I, only athletes from countries on the winning side were allowed to enter.

Berlin 1936

The Games in Berlin in 1936, just before World War II, were very controversial. Adolf Hitler and his Nazi Party intended using the Olympics to show the world the superiority of the Aryan race of people. The African-American athlete, Jessie Owens, won four gold medals and upset Hitler and the Nazis with his success.

Melbourne 1956

The water polo match between Hungary and the USSR became known as Blood in the Water because of the violence that occurred between the two teams. The Soviets had sent soldiers and tanks into Hungary the month before the Olympics. During the Olympics, some Hungarian athletes claimed political asylum in Australia.

Munich 1972

Terrorists murdered eleven members of the team from Israel. This shocking event cast a sad cloud over the Olympics that year.

Above: Olympia Park was constructed for the Munich 1972 Olympics Summer Games

Moscow 1980 and Los Angeles 1984

One of the most successful countries in the Olympics, the USA, did not send athletes to Moscow in 1980. The USA was showing its opposition to the invasion of Afghanistan by the USSR. At the next Olympics in Los Angeles, in 1984, the USSR refused to send any athletes. Australian officials also tried to stop local athletes going to the Moscow Olympics, but they did not succeed. The Australian team competed and won two gold medals in swimming.

Below: Members of the US Olympics Team as they march into the LA Coliseum during the 1984 Summer Olympics

Sydney 2000

There were a number of political events that marked the Sydney Olympics in 2000:

- The athletes from North and South Korea marched together, despite the political differences between their countries.
- Four athletes from East Timor represented their new country, but only as individuals, since East Timor had not yet officially achieved independence. The four men trained in Darwin as part of Australia's aid program to the new country.
- Taiwan competed as Chinese Taipei. The flag they used was designed especially for these Olympics.

Above: Chinese Taipei Olympic flag

Paralympics

Timeline for the History of the Paralympics

1948	Sir Ludwig Guttmann organised a sports competition in England for soldiers who had suffered a spinal injury in World War II.
1952	The next competition involved Dutch and British competitors. This was the beginning of the Paralympic Movement.
1960	The sporting competition for disabled athletes was first organised in an Olympic style at the Games in Rome.
1976	In the Toronto Games, a variety of disability groups were involved in the competitions.
1976	The first Paralympic Winter Games took place in Sweden.
1988	Since the Seoul Summer Olympics, the Summer Paralympics have been held at the same venue as the Olympics.
1992	Since the Albertville Winter Games, the Winter Paralympics have been held at the same venue as the Olympics.
2001	The IOC agreed that future bids to host the Olympic Games must also include hosting the Paralympics.

Sydney 2000 Paralympics

The torch relay commenced with a lighting ceremony at Parliament House in Canberra. Special medals were designed, opening and closing ceremonies were staged, and Lizzie the frill-necked lizard became the Sydney 2000 Paralympic mascot.

Australia topped the medal tally at the Sydney 2000 Paralympics, with disabled athletes winning a total of 149 medals. The outstanding performance was by Siobhan Paton, who won six swimming gold medals. Also notable for Australia was Tim Sullivan, who won five gold medals in athletics. Louise Sauvage, one of Australia's greatest athletes, won gold in wheelchair racing and also had the honour of lighting the cauldron.

Right: Lizzie the frill-necked lizard

Youth Olympic Games

The first Youth Olympic Games (YOG) were held in Singapore in 2010. The summer and winter Youth Olympics are held every four years and are organised in a similar way to the Olympic Games. They are for athletes aged fifteen to eighteen and their aim is to give young people experience in international competition. While activities and workshops help athletes learn about the Olympic values, the Youth Olympics give a role to non-athletes as well, encouraging young ambassadors, role models and reporters to become involved.

Symbols of the Youth Olympic Games

The first YOG mascots were Lyo and Merly for the Games in Singapore in 2010. In Nanjing four years later the mascot was called Nanjinglele.

Medals and Emblems

The host of the YOG produces a separate set of medals for winning athletes, and also their own emblem for the Games.

SUSTAINABILITY AND THE YOG

Organisers of the YOG are expected to follow these guidelines:

- ethical sourcing
- sustainable procurement methods
- delivering a sustainable legacy to the host city and its young people

Australia at the Youth Olympic Games

Australia has sent representatives to all the Youth Olympic Games. The athletes have won gold medals at the summer YOG and at the winter YOG in Lillehammer.

FIVE THEMES OF YOG

1. Olympism
2. Skills Development
3. Well-being and Healthy Lifestyle
4. Social Responsibility
5. Expression

SUMMER GAMES

Singapore 2010
Nanjing, China 2014
Buenos Aires, Argentina 2018

WINTER GAMES

Innsbruck, Austria 2012
Lillehammer, Norway 2016
Lausanne, Switzerland 2020

Australians at the Summer Olympic Games

Australia's increasing medal tally at the Olympic Games, particularly in swimming, led the world to think of Australia as a land of health, fitness, sunshine and beaches. This view was one of the factors that encouraged migrants from Europe to make Australia their new home after World War II.

Athens, Greece, 1896

The first modern Olympic Games were not followed as they are today, and in Australia very few people knew about them. Edwin Flack was living in London in 1896 and decided to compete in the Olympics. Australia was not a nation at this time, so Edwin was allowed to compete as a member of his old school club instead. He beat the American favourite to win the 1,500 metres running race. He also won the 800 metres race and competed in the marathon and in the tennis tournament. The first Games did not award gold medals so Edwin Flack received silver medals, which were the highest awarded at that time. His win was reported in the Sydney Morning Herald newspaper in a single line, without any further comment. Because of his decision to travel to Athens and compete, Australia can now claim to have had entrants in every modern Olympic Games held.

Paris, France, 1900

Freddie Lane was one of only three Australian athletes to attend these Olympics, and he won Australia's first gold medal in swimming. The race was held in the Seine River. He also won the obstacle race, in which swimmers had to climb over and swim under boats.

Australia's first medal for shooting was won by David Mackintosh. The disorganisation of these Paris Olympics resulted in his gold medal not being confirmed until 1987, after his death.

St Louis, USA, 1904

There was little interest in the Olympics and Australia sent only three athletes. Francis Gailey was the only medal winner, with three silver and one bronze in swimming.

Below: Preparation for the 100m race, 1896 Athens

London, Great Britain, 1908

Australia and New Zealand sent a combined team to these Olympics. They competed under the name Australasia. The rugby team, the Wallabies, were on a tour of Great Britain at the time, and only decided to enter the Olympics at the last minute. They won the gold medal but their only opponent was Great Britain. The Olympics were still not considered to be very important as an international sporting event, and Great Britain had not sent its best players to compete.

Stockholm, Sweden, 1912

Australia's first female athlete at the Olympics was Fanny Durack. She won a gold medal in swimming in an era when it was still controversial for a woman to be seen in public wearing a swimming costume. The two women in the team had to raise their own funds for travel and expenses for the Olympics. The other Australian female competitor, Mina Wylie, won the silver medal. In later years, Fanny Durack continued to lead the world in swimming, and held many freestyle world records. The men's relay team in swimming also won a gold medal at these Olympics, with one member being a New Zealander. As in 1908, Australians and New Zealanders competed as Australasia at Stockholm.

Antwerp, Belgium, 1920

The swimming events were held in a pool built in a canal. Australia did not win any gold medals, but Frank Beaurepaire won a bronze medal in swimming. He later founded a tyre business which is well-known throughout Australia.

Paris, France, 1924

Andrew 'Boy' Charlton set his first swimming world record at the age of fifteen. In the 1,500 metres freestyle swimming he won by forty metres and in record time. Competing against him from the USA was Johnny Weissmuller, who later played the role of Tarzan in a series of movies.

The first Australian to win a medal in athletics was Nick Winter. He won the gold medal and set a world record in what is now known as the triple jump. Australia's first Olympic gold medal for diving was won by Richmond Eve.

Above: Henry Pearce

Amsterdam, Holland, 1928

Henry Pearce was a champion rower and won Australia's only gold medal at these Olympics. The record he set was not beaten until 1972.

Los Angeles, USA, 1932

Edgar Gray competed in three Olympic Games. In 1932 he won the gold medal for cycling, even though he was not well on the day of the race. He had grown up cycling to and from school and won many Australian cycling titles.

Clare Dennis won a gold medal in swimming. It was a very close race and she set a world record. These were the second Olympics for Henry Pearce, and he won gold again in rowing.

Above: Frank Beaurepaire

Berlin, Germany, 1936

Australians won no gold medals at the Berlin Olympics, even though there was a large team of athletes. These were the Olympics at which Hitler refused to congratulate any of the African American athletes.

London, Great Britain, 1948

Not distracted by the fact that a running race was being held at the same time in the stadium, John Winter won a gold medal in the high jump. Merv Wood, who later became the NSW Police Commissioner, won a gold medal in rowing.

Helsinki, Finland, 1952

One of Australia's greatest athletes, Marjorie Jackson, won two gold medals in running at these Olympics. Another Australian athlete, Shirley Strickland, won a gold medal in the hurdles.

John Davies won a gold medal in swimming, and Russell Mockridge won two gold medals, one in individual cycling and one with Lionel Cox in tandem cycling. Lionel Cox had never ridden a tandem bicycle before going to Helsinki. Shortly after this triumph, he also won a silver medal in the cycling sprint.

Above: Shirley Strickland

Melbourne, Australia, 1956

Australians were proud that their country was the first outside Europe and the USA to host the Olympics. Local athletes excelled, but the crowds cheered enthusiastically for all the competitors.

Gold medals were won by Betty Cuthbert, Shirley Strickland, Lorraine Crapp, Dawn Fraser, Jon Hendricks, Murray Rose, David Thiele, as well as the Australian teams for the tandem cycling, athletics relay, men's swimming relay and women's swimming relay. The silver and bronze medal tallies were also impressive. The gold medallists became household names throughout Australia for many years after these Olympics were over.

Rome, Italy, 1960

The Australian equestrian team surprised Australia by winning a gold medal, even though one of the competitors had injured his arm and had it in a sling. One of the team members, Laurie Morgan, also won an individual gold medal. John Devitt, Dawn Fraser, John Conrads, Murray Rose and David Thiele all succeeded in the pool, and Herb Elliott won a gold medal in running, winning by twenty metres.

Above: Betty Cuthbert

Tokyo, Japan, 1964

Dawn Fraser combined a gold medal win with controversy about her choice of swimsuit and her souveniring of a flag. Betty Cuthbert was not expected to win but delighted Australians with another gold medal in running. The yachting team won Australia's first gold medal in this sport, with Bill Northam becoming Australia's oldest gold medal winner at fifty nine years old.

Above: Herb Elliott

Mexico City, Mexico, 1968

The high altitude was a problem for many of the athletes but, despite this, Australians won a total of seventeen medals. Ron Clarke, the distance runner, collapsed due to the altitude and became very ill. Just before these Olympics began, hundreds of student protestors were killed when Mexican authorities fired on them. This dampened the mood of the Games for many of the athletes and spectators.

Munich, Germany, 1972

When terrorists killed eleven members of the team from Israel, the Olympics were halted for a day of mourning. The IOC decided not to cancel the Games altogether, and Australian athletes once again excelled in swimming, with Shane Gould winning three gold medals.

Montreal, Canada, 1976

Australians could barely believe that their athletes did not bring home any gold medals from these Games. As a result, the Australian Institute of Sport was established. Its aim was to give athletes professional training and prepare them for future competitions.

Moscow, USSR, 1980

Soviet troops had invaded Afghanistan just months before the Olympics, and fifty-six countries refused to attend as a result. Most of the Australian athletes decided to attend and they won two gold medals in swimming.

Los Angeles, USA, 1984

Australian athletes won twenty-four medals, including four gold. Dean Lukin's gold for weight lifting was achieved even though he only trained part-time. During the summer he was a tuna fisherman.

Seoul, South Korea, 1988

The disqualification of Canadian, Ben Johnson, for using performance enhancing drugs, made the world aware that drugs had now become a part of international sport. Debbie Flintoff-King ran an exciting hurdles race, winning gold by only hundredths of a second.

Barcelona, Spain, 1992

Kieren Perkins won the only swimming gold medal for Australia at these Games. Six gold medals were won in cycling, canoeing, equestrian events and rowing.

Atlanta, USA, 1996

Australians won forty-one medals, including nine gold. Cathy Freeman won a silver medal in the 400 metres running race, the same event in which she was to win her famous gold medal four years later in Sydney.

Above: Grant Hackett in Barcelona

Above: Australian cycling team, Athens

Sydney, Australia, 2000

Australian athletes achieved the highest medal tally ever at these Olympics. People living in Sydney observed the massive preparations, as venues were built all around the city. Residents were encouraged to be welcoming to visitors. Even in suburbs away from the venues, local councils painted signs on the roads to alert pedestrians to look right before walking across. This was because so many of the visitors would come from countries where cars drove on the opposite side of the road and they were accustomed to looking to the left to check for traffic. Australia won an impressive fifty-eight medals at these Olympics, including sixteen gold.

Athens, Greece, 2004

In his second Olympic Games, swimmer Ian Thorpe won two gold medals. The cyclists won six gold medals, making Australians realise that they had top cyclists who, up until then, were not well known by the general public. Australia won seventeen gold medals at these Games, with sixteen silver and sixteen bronze.

Beijing, China, 2008

China was keen to show the world that it could host an outstanding Olympic Games and provide exceptional facilities. The Bird's Nest stadium amazed everyone who saw it, whether in person or on television. Australia came sixth in the international total medal tally at these Olympics, with fourteen gold medals, while China itself came second after the USA.

London, Great Britain, 2012

There were no individual swimming gold medals at these Olympics, but the three gold medals won in sailing showed the world that Australia could be a formidable force in this sport.

Rio De Janeiro, Brazil, 2016

After initial concerns about the spread of the Zika virus and whether the venues would be completed in time, the Rio Olympic Games eventually ran smoothly. Some Russian athletes were banned from competing due to concerns over the use of performance enhancement drugs. Incidents of petty theft and disputes with authorities in Rio plagued the Australian team and many commentators complained that their gold medal tally was not as high as expected. Australia came tenth in the overall medal tally. The women's rugby sevens team made history when they won the gold medal for the first ever rugby sevens event at the Olympics.

Above: Sailing in the London Olympics
Below: Rio Olympics

Australian Gold Medal Winners
at the Summer Olympic Games

YEAR	ATHLETE	EVENT
1896 - I Athens, Greece	Edwin Flack	800m and 1500m
1900 - II Paris, France	Fred Lane	Swimming - 200m Freestyle and 200m Obstacle Race
	David Mackintosh	Shooting
1904 - III St Louis, USA	No gold medals won by Australia	
1908 - IV London, Great Britain	John Barnett, Phillip Carmichael, Daniel Carroll, Robert Craig, Thomas Griffin, John Hickey, Malcolm McArthur, Arthur McCabe, Patrick McCue, Christopher McKivat (captain), Charles McMurtrie, Sydney Middleton, Thomas Richards, Charles Russell, Frank Smith	Rugby Union
1912 - V Stockholm, Sweden	Sarah Durack	Swimming - 100m Freestyle
1916 - VI	Games cancelled due to Word War I	
1920 - VII Antwerp, Belgium	No gold medals won by Australia	
1924 - VIII Paris, France	Anthony Winter	Athletics - Triple Jump
	Richmond Eve	Diving - Plain Tower
	Andrew 'Boy' Charlton	Swimming - 1500m Freestyle
1928 - IX Amsterdam, Netherlands	Henry 'Bobby' Pearce	Rowing - Single Scull
1932 - X Los Angeles, USA	Edgar 'Dunc' Gray	Cycling - 1000m Time Trial
	Henry 'Bobby' Pearce	Rowing - Single Scull
	Clare Dennis	Swimming - 200m Breaststroke
1936 - XI Berlin, Germany	No gold medals won by Australia	
1940 - XII	Games cancelled due to Word War II	
1944 - XIII	Games cancelled due to Word War II	
1948 - XIV London, Great Britain	John Winter	Athletics - High Jump
	Mervyn Wood	Rowing - Single Scull
1952 - XV Helsinki, Finland	Marjorie Jackson	Athletics - 100m and 200m
	Shirley Strickland	Athletics - 80m Hurdles
	Russell Mockridge	Cycling - 1000m Time Trial
	Lionel Cox and Russell Mockridge	Cycling - 2000m Tandem
	John Davies	Swimming - 200m Breaststroke
1956 - XVI Melbourne, Australia	Betty Cuthbert	Athletics - 100m and 200m
	Shirley Strickland	Athletics - 80m Hurdles
	Norma Croker, Betty Cuthbert, Fleur Mellor, Shirley Strickland	Athletics - 4 x 100m Relay
	Ian Browne, Anthony Marchant	Cycling - 2000m Tandem
	Lorraine Crapp	Swimming - 400m Freestyle
	Dawn Fraser	Swimming - 100m Freestyle
	Jon Henricks	Swimming - 100m Freestyle
	Murray Rose	Swimming - 400m and 1500m Freestyle
	David Theile	Swimming - 100m Backstroke
1960 - XVII Rome, Italy	John Devitt, Jon Henricks, Kevin O'Halloran, Murray Rose	Swimming - 4 x 200m Freestyle Relay
	Lorraine Crapp, Dawn Fraser, Faith Leech, Sandra Morgan	Swimming - 4 x 100m Freestyle Relay
	Betty Cuthbert	Athletics - 400m
1964 - XVIII Tokyo, Japan	Kevin Berry	Swimming - 200m Butterfly
	Dawn Fraser	Swimming - 100m Freestyle
	Ian O'Brien	Swimming - 200m Breaststroke
	Robert Windle	Swimming - 1500m Freestyle
	William Northam, Peter O'Donnell, Dick Sargeant	Yachting - 5.5 Metre Class

YEAR	ATHLETE	EVENT
1968 - XIX Mexico City, Mexico	Maureen Caird	Athletics - 80m Hurdles
	Ralph Doubell	Athletics - 800m
	Lynette McClements	Swimming - 100m Butterfly
	Michael Wenden	Swimming - 100m Freestyle and 200m Freestyle
1972 - XX Munich, West Germany	Brad Cooper	Swimming - 400m Freestyle
	Shane Gould	Swimming - 200m and 400m Freestyle, 200m Individual Medley
	Gail Neall	Swimming - 400m Individual Medley
	Beverley Whitfield	Swimming - 200m Breaststroke
	Thomas Anderson, John Cuneo, John Shaw	Yachting - Dragon Class
	John Anderson, David Forbes	Yachting - Star Class
1976 - XXI Montreal, Canada	No gold medals won by Australia	
1980 - XXII Moscow, USSR	Michelle Ford	Swimming - 800m Freestyle
	Neil Brooks, Peter Evans, Mark Kerry, Mark Tonelli	Swimming - 4x100m Medley Relay
1984 - XXIII Los Angeles, USA	Glynis Nunn	Athletics - Heptathlon
	Michael Grenda, Kevin Nichols, Michael Turtur, Dean Woods	Cycling - 4000m Team Pursuit
	Jon Sieben	Swimming - 200m Butterfly
	Dean Lukin	Weightlifting - Super Heavyweight 110kg+
1988 - XXIV Seoul, Korea	Debbie Flintoff-King	Athletics - 400m Hurdles
	Tracy Belbin, Deborah Bowman, Michelle Capes, Lee Capes, Sally Carbon, Elspeth Clement, Loretta Dorman, Maree Fish, Rechelle Hawkes, Lorraine Hillas, Kathleen Partridge, Sharon Buchanan, Jacqueline Pereira, Sandra Pisani, Kim Small, Liane Tooth	Hockey (women)
	Duncan Armstrong	Swimming - 200m Freestyle
1992 - XXV Barcelona, Spain	Clint Robinson	Canoe / Kayak - K1 1000m
	Kathryn Watt	Cycling - Individual Road Race
	Matthew Ryan	Equestrian - Three Day Event Individual
	Andrew Hoy, Gillian Rolton, Matthew Ryan	Equestrian - Three Day Event Team
	Peter Antonie, Stephen Hawkins	Rowing - Double Sculls
	Andrew Cooper, Nicholas Green, Michael McKay, James Tomkins	Rowing - Coxless Four
	Kieren Perkins	Swimming - 1500m Freestyle
1996 - XXVI Atlanta, USA	Phillip Dutton, Andrew Hoy, Gillian Rolton, Wendy Schaeffer	Equestrian - Three Day Event Team
	Michelle Andrews, Alyson Annan, Louise Dobson, Renita Farrell, Juliet Haslam, Rechelle Hawkes, Clover Maitland, Karen Marsden, Jennifer Morris, Jacqueline Pereira, Nova Peris, Katrina Powell, Lisa Carruthers (Powell), Danielle Roche, Kate Starre, Liane Tooth	Hockey (women)
	Drew Ginn, Nicholas Green, Michael McKay, James Tomkins	Rowing - Coxless Four
	Kate Slatter, Megan Stil	Rowing - Coxless Pair
	Michael Diamond	Shooting - Trap
	Russell Mark	Shooting - Double Trap
	Susan O'Neill	Swimming - 200m Butterfly
	Kieren Perkins	Swimming - 1500m Freestyle
	Todd Woodbridge, Mark Woodforde	Tennis - Doubles
2000 - XXVII Sydney, Australia	Simon Fairweather	Archery - Individual
	Catherine Freeman	Athletics - 400m
	Brett Aitken, Scott McGrory	Cycling - Madison
	Phillip Dutton, Andrew Hoy, Matthew Ryan, Stuart Tinney	Equestrian - Three Day Event Team
	Katie Allen, Alyson Annan, Lisa Carruthers (Powell), Renita Garard, Juliet Haslam, Rechelle Hawkes, Nicole Hudson, Rachel Imison, Clover Maitland, Claire Mitchell-Taverner, Jennifer Morris, Alison Peek, Katrina Powell, Angela Skirving, Kate Starre, Julie Towers	Hockey (women)
	Thomas King, Mark Turnbull	Sailing - 470 Class
	Jennifer Armstrong, Belinda Stowel	Sailing - 470 Class
	Michael Diamond	Shooting - Trap
	Grant Hackett	Swimming - 1500m Freestyle
	Susan O'Neill	Swimming - 200m Freestyle
	Ian Thorpe	Swimming - 400m Freestyle
	Ashley Callus, Chris Fydler, Michael Klim, Ian Thorpe, Todd Pearson, Adam Pine	Swimming - 4 x 100m Freestyle Relay
	William Kirby, Michael Klim, Todd Pearson, Ian Thorpe, Grant Hackett, Daniel Kowalski	Swimming - 4 x 200m Freestyle Relay
	Lauren Burns	Taekwondo - Under 49 kg
	Natalie Cook, Kerri-Ann Pottharst	Volleyball (beach)

YEAR	ATHLETE	EVENT
	Naomi Castle, Joanne Fox, Bridgette Gusterson, Simone Hankin, Yvette Higgins, Kate Hooper, Bronwyn Mayer, Gail Miller, Melissa Mills, Debbie Watson, Elizabeth Weekes, Danielle Woodhouse, Taryn Woods	Water Polo (women)
2004 - XXVIII Athens, Greece	Sara Carrigan	Cycling - Individual Road Race
	Ryan Bayley	Cycling - Sprint and Keirin
	Graeme Brown, Luke Roberts, Brett Lancaster, Brad McGee, Peter Dawson, Stephen Wooldridge	Cycling - 4000m Team Pursuit
	Graeme Brown, Stuart O'Grady	Cycling - Madison
	Anna Meares	Cycling - 500m Time Trial
	Chantelle Newbery	Diving - 10m Platform
	Michael Brennan, Travis Brooks, Dean Butler, Liam de Young, Jamie Dwyer, Nathan Eglington, Troy Elder, Bevan George, Robert Hammond, Mark Hickman, Mark Knowles, Brent Livermore, Michael McCann, Stephen Mowlam, Grant Schubert, Matthew Wells	Hockey (men)
	Drew Ginn, James Tomkins	Rowing - Pair
	Suzanne Balogh	Shooting - Trap
	Jodie Henry	Swimming - 100m Freestyle
	Petria Thomas	Swimming - 100m Butterfly
	Ian Thorpe	Swimming - 200m Freestyle and 400m Freestyle
	Grant Hackett	Swimming - 1500m Freestyle
	Jodie Henry, Lisbeth Lenton, Alice Mills, Petria Thomas, Sarah Ryan	Swimming - 4 x 100m Freestyle Relay
	Giaan Rooney, Petria Thomas, Leisel Jones, Jodie Henry, Brooke Hanson, Alice Mills, Jessicah Schipper	Swimming - 4 x 100m Medley Relay
2008 - XXIX Beijing, China	Steven Hooker	Athletics - Pole Vault
	Ken Wallace	Canoe/Kayak - K1 500m
	Matthew Mitcham	Diving - 10m Platform
	Scott Brennan, David Crawshay	Rowing - Double Sculls
	Duncan Free, Drew Ginn	Rowing - Pair
	Tessa Parkinson, Elise Rechichi	Sailing - Two Person Dinghy 470
	Malcolm Page, Nathan Wilmot	Sailing - Two Person Dinghy 470
	Leisel Jones	Swimming - 100m Breaststroke
	Lisbeth Trickett	Swimming - 100m Butterfly
	Stephanie Rice	Swimming - 400m Individual Medley and 200m Individual Medley
	Stephanie Rice, Bronte Barratt, Kylie Palmer, Linda MacKenzie, Felicity Galvez, Angie Bainbridge, Melanie Schlanger, Lara Davenport	Swimming - 4 x 200m Freestyle Relay
	Emily Seebohm, Leisel Jones, Jessicah Schipper, Lisbeth Trickett (Lenton), Tarnee White, Felicity Galvez, Shayne Reese	Swimming - 4 x 100m Medley Relay
	Emma Snowsill	Triathlon
2012 - XXX London, Great Britain	Sally Pearson	Athletics - 100m hurdles
	Jacob Clear, Murray Stewart, Tate Smith, David Smith	Canoe/Kayak - K4 1000m
	Anna Meares	Cycling - Individual Sprint
	Malcolm Page, Mathew Belcher	Sailing - Two Person Dinghy 470
	Thomas Slingsby	Sailing - Laser
	Iain Jensen, Nathan Outteridge	Sailing - 49er
	Cate Campbell, Alicia Coutts, Brittany Elmslie, Melanie Schlanger, Lisbeth Trickett, Yolane Kukla, Emily Seebohm	Swimming - 4 x 100m Freestyle Relay
2016 - XXXI Rio De Janeiro, Brazil	Nicole Beck, Charlotte Caslick, Emilee Cherry, Chloe Dalton, Gemma Etheridge, Ellia Green, Shannon Parry, Evania Pelite, Alicia Quirk, Emma Tonegato, Amy Turner, Sharni Williams	Women's Rugby Sevens
	Kimberley Brennan	Rowing - Single Skulls
	Tom Barton	Sailing - Men's Laser
	Cate Campbell, Bronte Campbell, Brittany Elmslie, Emma McKeon, Madison Wilson	Swimming - 4 x 100m Freestyle
	Kyle Chalmers	Swimming - 100m Freestyle
	Mack Horton	Swimming - 400m Freestyle
	Chloe Esposito	Modern Pentathlon
	Catherine Skinner	Shooting - Women's Trap

Australians at the Winter Olympic Games

The first Winter Olympic Games were held in Chamonix, France in 1924, and all the Winter Olympics since then have been held in the northern hemisphere. They were originally held in the same year as the Summer Olympics but in 1994 the IOC decided that they should be held two years apart.

The mascots chosen for the Winter Games are usually animals that live in snow and ice, or cartoon characters representing life in cold climates. For the 1960 Winter Olympics in Squaw Valley, USA, Walt Disney was appointed head of the committee to organise the opening ceremony. His theatrical approach set the scene for all future opening ceremonies.

Australians have competed in every Winter Olympics since 1936, except for those held in St Moritz in 1948.

In the 1990s, Australia's performance improved after the creation of the Olympic Winter Institute of Australia and the purchase of a training base in Austria.

Right: Chantelle Kerry figure skating, Austria Winter Olympics 2012
Below: Australian bobsleigh team, Sochi Winter Olympics 2014

Lillehammer, Norway, 1994

Australia's first ever Winter Olympics medal was a bronze in the men's 5,000 metres short track relay speed skating event.

Nagano, Japan, 1998

Zali Steggall won a bronze medal in the slalom event. This was Australia's first individual medal at a Winter Olympics.

Salt Lake City, USA, 2002

These Winter Olympics marked a turning point for Australia. Two athletes won gold medals, the first ever won for Australia. Steven Bradbury won the 1,000 metres short track speed skating slalom event after all the other competitors were involved in a pile-up. Alisa Camplin won the aerials event.

Above: David Morris, freestyle skiing, Sochi Olympics 2014

Above: Dale Begg-Smith, mens moguls, Sochi Olympics 2014

Turin, Italy, 2006

Dale Begg-Smith won the gold medal in the men's freestyle moguls skiing. Alisa Camplin claimed her second Olympic medal, a bronze in the aerials event.

Vancouver, Canada, 2010

Torah Bright won a gold medal in the women's half-pipe snowboarding, Lydia Lassila won a gold medal in the aerial freestyle skiing, and Dale Begg-Smith won a silver in the moguls.

Sochi, Russia, 2014

Australia sent its largest ever winter team to the Sochi Winter Olympics, with sixty athletes attending. David Morris won a silver medal in aerial skiing, Torah Bright won a silver medal in the half-pipe snowboard, and Lydia Lassila won a bronze medal in aerial skiing.

Locations of all the Winter Olympic Games

1924, Chamonix, France
1928, St Moritz, Switzerland
1932, Lake Placid, USA
1936, Garmisch-Partenkirchen, Germany
1940 & 1944, Cancelled due to World War II
1948, St Moritz, Switzerland
1952, Oslo, Norway
1956, Cortina d'Ampezzo, Italy
1960, Squaw Valley, USA
1964, Innsbruck, Austria
1968, Grenoble, France
1972, Sapporo, Japan
1976, Innsbruck, Austria
1980, Lake Placid, USA
1984, Sarajevo, Yugoslavia
1988, Calgary, Canada
1992, Albertville, France
1994, Lillehammer, Norway
1998, Nagano, Japan
2002, Salt Lake City, USA
2006, Turin, Italy
2010, Vancouver, Canada
2014, Sochi, Russia
2018, Pyeongchang, South Korea

Glossary

WORD	MEANING
consecutive	following each other
distinguished	dignified
eventing	riders and horses taking part in several events
livestock	farm animals
political asylum	protection for a person when they are escaping a political threat
quarantine	keeping animals separated in case they are carrying diseases
to submerge	to place underwater
wreath	circle of leaves or flowers

Where to find out more about the Olympic Games

www.olympic.org
www.olympics.com.au
www.sopa.nsw.gov.au
www.paralympic.org
www.corporate.olympics.com.au

Index